Classic Recipes of
SINGAPORE

Classic Recipes of

SINGAPORE

TRADITIONAL FOOD AND COOKING IN 25 AUTHENTIC DISHES

GHILLIE BAŞAN

PHOTOGRAPHY BY WILLIAM LINGWOOD

LORENZ BOOKS

This edition is published by
Lorenz Books,
an imprint of Anness Publishing Ltd,
108 Great Russell Street,
London WC1B 3NA

www.lorenzbooks.com;
www.annesspublishing.com

© Anness Publishing Limited 2014

If you like the images in this book and
would like to investigate using them for
publishing, promotions or advertising,
please visit our website
www.practicalpictures.com for more
information.

Publisher: Joanna Lorenz
Editor: Doreen Gillon & Helen Sudell
Designer: Nigel Partridge
Recipe Photography: William Lingwood
Home Economists: Lucy McKelvie &
 Bridget Sargeson
Stylist: Helen Trent
Production Controller: Pirong Wang

A CIP catalogue record for this book is
available from the British Library

PUBLISHER'S NOTE
Although the advice and information in this
book are believed to be accurate and true
at the time of going to press, neither the
authors nor the publisher can accept any
legal responsibility or liability for any errors
or omissions that may have been made nor
for any inaccuracies nor for any loss, harm
or injury that comes about from following
instructions or advice in this book.

These recipes were originally published as
part of a larger volume, *The Food and
Cooking of Malaysia & Singapore*.

PUBLISHER'S ACKNOWLEDGEMENTS
The Publisher would like to thank the
following agencies for the use of their
images. Alamy: p10 (both), p11tr.
Fotalia: p9. Istock: p6, p8.

COOK'S NOTES
Bracketed terms are intended for American
readers. For all recipes, quantities are given
in both metric and imperial measures and,
where appropriate, in standard cups and
spoons. Follow one set of measures, but
not a mixture, because they are not
interchangeable.

Standard spoon and cup measures are
level. 1 tsp = 5ml, 1 tbsp = 15ml, 1 cup =
250ml/8fl oz. Australian standard
tablespoons are 20ml. Australian readers
should use 3 tsp in place of 1 tbsp for
measuring small quantities.

American pints are 16fl oz/2 cups.
American readers should use 20fl oz/2.5
cups in place of 1 pint when measuring
liquids.

Electric oven temperatures in this book are
for conventional ovens. When using a fan
oven, the temperature will probably need to
be reduced by about 10–20°C/20–40°F.
Since ovens vary, you should check with
your manufacturer's instruction book for
guidance.

The nutritional analysis given for each
recipe is calculated per portion (i.e. serving
or item), unless otherwise stated. If the
recipe gives a range, such as Serves 4–6,
then the nutritional analysis will be for the
smaller portion size, i.e. 6 servings. The
analysis does not include optional
ingredients, such as salt added to taste.

Medium (US large) eggs are used unless
otherwise stated.

Contents

Introduction

The rich variety of culinary traditions found throughout South-east Asia come together in the small independent nation of Singapore. With a population of 76 per cent Chinese, 15 per cent Malay and 6 per cent Indian, with a small number of Peranakan, Eurasian and Indonesian peoples, the result is one of the most colourful and exciting cuisines in the world. This is made all the more tangible with the famous Singaporean hawker stalls, where exotic food from each of these cultures can be sampled in one place.

Left: The beautiful twin pagodas reflected in the quiet waters of Jorong Lake in Singapore's Chinese Garden.

Singaporean Cuisine

Often referred to as the "Manhattan of the East", Singapore is a consumer's paradise and food is a national obsession. Singapore is rich in diverse cultures and food traditions, but to many Singaporeans the origin of the dish is unimportant as long as it is tasty. Chinese food rules the roost, followed closely by Malay and Indian.

With no agriculture but a great deal of affluence, so that many goods can be imported, the cuisine of the tiny nation

Below: Chilli crab is one of Singapore's signature dishes.

has developed from the simple barrow on the street corner, selling one single dish cooked on a burner, to some of the most sophisticated hawker stalls in the world.

The hawker tradition and coffee shop (*kopi tiam* – similar to a Western café) culture are most popular in Singapore, as many people are busy and live in tiny apartments, so eating out is the obvious choice. For some, cooking at home is only a weekend activity. As Singapore is divided into racial quarters, the hawker stalls and coffee shops follow a similar pattern. In Katong, the Peranakan and Eurasian section, they offer competitive versions of Singapore laksa, noodles in coconut milk, right next to coffee shops selling European tea cakes or Chinese chicken rice cafés. In Little India, the warm, spicy aromas of the Tekka Market attract Hindu, Muslim and Chinese shoppers, as well as the *nonyas* (Peranakan ladies) and European *taitais* (ladies of

leisure) who descend on the Indian coffee shops to tuck into a freshly made *roti paratha* (flaky flatbread), taken with the sweet pulled tea, *teh tarik*.

Unique to Singapore are the dosai shops, which sell Indian rice crêpes, dosai, and vegetarian dishes, as they are run by Hindus who do not eat meat. In the same areas you will find Indian "banana leaf" restaurants, where the food is served on banana leaves.

While there are only slight differences between dishes such as Singapore and Penang *laksa*, or Johor and Singapore *char kway teow*, some dishes are unique to Singapore – they are often versions of traditional dishes that have been given a Singapore twist. One that has become a Singapore classic is stir-fried chilli crab in a tomato sauce, eaten with the fingers and mopped up with bread.

Right: Shopping for fresh ingredients is an integral part of life in Singapore.

Feasts and Festivals

With such a variety of culinary cultures, every religious or family celebration is a banquet of delights. Traditional weddings involve a great deal of feasting, some of which is symbolic and can last several days. In Singapore, births also require ceremonial feasting, which often takes place on the 100th day in Chinese households.

Weddings

A Malay wedding in Singapore is a huge affair with hundreds of guests being served rice dishes and curries. As they depart, each guest is presented with

Below: A Malay bridal couple, resplendent in traditional dress.

delicately wrapped gifts of hard-boiled eggs to ensure fertility for the newly-weds. Similarly, Indian weddings operate on a large scale with a vast selection of dishes tailored to the religious groups.

Chinese weddings are more restrained with a traditional tea ceremony and a family banquet.

Christmas

It may not snow at Christmas in Singapore but there is no shortage of fake snow, twinkling lights, furs, shiny baubles and silver tinsel. Christmas may be a Eurasian festival, but everyone joins in. In Eurasian households, roast turkey is served, stuffed with glutinous rice, pork and chestnuts. Honey-baked hams are accompanied by chicken or pork curries. With such a colourful European and Malay heritage in Singapore, the Eurasians draw from all their influences at Christmas, adding soy-based dishes, chilli dips, cabbage rolls, fruitcakes and sponge cakes to the feast. As most Eurasians are Catholic,

Above: Brightly coloured sweets are very popular at New Year.

they attend midnight mass on Christmas Eve and return home to the table laden with the festive delicacies.

Chinese New Year

Shortly after Christmas, preparations for the Chinese New Year begin. Traditionally, this festival marked the advent of spring for the Chinese farmers, but for the urban Chinese, the event represents a spiritual renewal rather than a physical one. On New Year's Day orange segments are presented to guests for good fortune, and candies are offered to ensure a sweet future.

On the seventh day of the New Year, Chinese families eat *yu sheng*, a traditional salad of finely sliced raw fish, tossed with shredded vegetables, candied melon, pomelo segments, strips of jellyfish, peanuts, sesame seeds and lime juice, which they believe will bring them prosperity.

Hari Raya Puasa

The third major festival on the calendar marks the end of Ramadan, the Muslim month of fasting and abstaining from other sensory pleasures between dawn and dusk. For

Below: Indian flatbreads are offered during the Diwali festival.

the men, the day begins with prayers in the mosques and then on to the cemeteries to pay respects to dead relatives.

The women prepare the feast at home, making rendang, beef cooked in coconut milk, which is served with *ketupat*, rice cakes, and *serunding*, a side dish of grated coconut fried with chilli. Once the meal has been consumed, friends and family visit one another, bearing gifts of cooked food, cakes and sweetmeats, which are enjoyed with endless cups of tea and coffee, or syrupy drinks.

Above: Christmas decorations in the famous Raffles Hotel.

Diwali

A Hindu celebration, the Festival of Lights marks the triumph of good over evil. It takes place on the rising of the new moon on the seventh month of the Hindu calendar, when oil lamps and candles are lit in family homes to welcome Lakshmi, the goddess of wealth. To celebrate, a wonderful array of vindaloo and biryani dishes, flatbreads and chutneys are prepared for friends and family.

Classic Ingredients

The air in some sections of the markets in Singapore is heady with the scents of the herb and spice stalls. Malay and Peranakan herb stalls include pungent roots, like ginger, galangal, lemon grass stalks, wild fern fronds and betal leaves for chewing. Equally alluring are the warm aromas from the Indian spice stalls, composed of cinnamon bark, star anise, fennel and cumin seeds, cardamom pods, cloves, ground turmeric and roasted curry powders. Other stalls are laden with dried goods, oils and condiments.

Below: A selection of spices used in Singaporean cooking.

The Singapore kitchen

Most Singaporean kitchen storecupboards have a supply of frequently used dried goods, seasonings, flavourings and condiments, such as candlenuts, cans of coconut milk, dried red chillies, packets of dried shrimp and the pungent shrimp paste, *belacan*, palm sugar, tamarind pulp, rice, dried egg noodles and a collection of spices.

Chinese kitchens also keep stocks of canned bamboo shoots and water chestnuts, dried shiitake mushrooms, salted duck eggs, Chinese cooking wine, called *shao shing*, Sichuan pepper, Chinese five-spice powder and bottles of hoisin sauce, which is made from salted soya beans, sugar, vinegar, sesame oil and spices.

Chilli sauce, soy sauces, sesame or groundnut (peanut) oil, and oyster sauce are stocked in most kitchens, while garlic, shallots, ginger, lemon grass, pandanus leaves, fresh coriander (cilantro) and fresh chillies are bought regularly from the markets.

Locally produced tomato ketchup appears in sauces for deep-fried seafood, sweet and sour dishes, Singapore chilli crab, and the Malay and Indian noodle dish, *mee goreng*. Hawkers liberally use tomato ketchup to flavour everything from Chinese noodles to Western-style fast food. Another versatile condiment is *kecap manis*, which is a thick soy sauce, sweetened with palm sugar, and used in the noodle dish, *char kway teow*.

Coconut also plays a key role. The freshly grated flesh appears in many dishes and the extracted water is used for braising and marinating. Most important, the fresh milk and cream extracted from the pulp are an integral part of many soups, noodle and rice dishes, curries and desserts.

Right: Coconut in all its forms features in many classic Singaporean dishes, from seafood laksa to ice cream.

Above: Chillies are an essential ingredient in Singapore.

Chillies galore

It is impossible to imagine a meal in Singapore without chillies. Pounded with other spices, using a mortar and pestle, chillies play a star part in the spice paste, *rempah*, which forms an integral part of Malay and Peranakan curries. As the Malays and Peranakans enjoy their food with a fiery blast, chillies are often added as a garnish, or as a side dish, to munch on while enjoying the already fiery curry or soupy noodles. Red chillies add heat and colour to a dish, whereas the green chillies tend to be

sliced on the side or pickled. Apart from adding a punch to several dishes, chillies form the basis of most sambals, which the Malays and Peranakans couldn't live without. Bird's eye chillies, *cili padi*, burn the tongue and throat the most, bringing tears to the eyes. Dried red chillies lack the pungency of fresh ones, but retain the heat and colour. Often, they are soaked in water until soft and pounded to a paste before being added to sauces and marinades. Chilli oil is drizzled over noodles, eggs and grilled and fried dishes.

Rempah is the heart and soul of Malay curries, soups and noodle dishes. It is also the foundation of many Nonya and Peranakan dishes found all over Singapore. Best prepared using a solid mortar and pestle, wet ingredients such as shallots, garlic, fresh ginger and turmeric, lemon grass stalks and chillies are pounded to a paste, followed by dry spices such as cinnamon, coriander seeds, cumin and candlenuts. Rempah

Above: The spice paste rempah is used in curries and sauces.

is then stir-fried in oil to release the natural oils and fragrance before adding the other ingredients. It performs the essential function of giving the dish a rich depth of flavour, as well as thickening the sauce.

Essential condiments

In Singapore the Malays and Indians often serve a selection of condiments with every meal. Most popular is the Malay Sambal Belacan and myriad Indian pickles or chutneys, all of which can be interchanged with the spicy food of this fascinating culture.

Pineapple pickle

This spicy sweet-and-sour pickle is ideal to serve with spicy grilled foods or as an accompaniment to curries or vegetable dishes.

Serves 6–8

15ml/1 tbsp brown mustard seeds
2 dried chillies, soaked in water until soft, seeded, and squeezed dry
15g/½oz fresh root ginger, peeled and chopped
1 garlic clove, chopped
5ml/1 tsp ground turmeric
200ml/7fl oz/scant 1 cup white wine vinegar or rice vinegar
15ml/1 tbsp palm sugar
1 ripe pineapple, peeled, cored and diced
salt

1 In a small, heavy pan, dry-roast the mustard seeds until they pop.

2 Grind the chillies, ginger and garlic to a paste. Stir in the mustard seeds and ground turmeric. Add the vinegar and sugar, stirring until the sugar has completely dissolved.

3 Put the pineapple in a bowl and pour over the pickling sauce. Add salt to taste. The pickle will keep for 2–3 days in the refrigerator.

Sambal belacan

This is the ubiquitous condiment of the Malays and Peranakans. A little dollop seems to go with everything: chunks of bread, rice, grilled foods, and stir-fried vegetables.

Serves 4

15ml/1 tbsp shrimp paste
4 fresh red chillies, seeded (reserve the seeds)
2 kaffir lime leaves, spines removed, and chopped
2.5ml/½ tsp sugar
1.5ml/¼ tsp salt
juice of 1 lime
1 lime, quartered, to serve

1 In a small, heavy pan, dry-roast the shrimp paste until it is aromatic and crumbly. Grind the roasted shrimp paste with the chillies to form a paste. Grind in half the chilli seeds and the lime leaves.

2 Add the sugar and salt, and stir in the rest of the chilli seeds. Moisten with the lime juice. Spoon the sambal into little dishes and serve with wedges of lime to squeeze over it.

COOK'S TIP

The fermented shrimp paste, belacan, is available in South-east Asian markets. If you cannot get hold of it, replace it with the readily available Thai shrimp paste.

Tastes of South-east Asia

The food and cooking of Singapore is steeped in the rich diversity of its people. Its vibrant mix of culinary traditions is celebrated here with delicious broths and soups, hot snacks and nourishing rice and noodle dishes. Other recipes highlight a passion for hot and spicy fish, sizzling meat, pickled vegetables and fragrant salads. Finally, an irresistible selection of sweet snacks and drinks complete this evocative collection of recipes which represent the very best food that Singapore has to offer.

Left: Fresh and dried chilies, galangal, turmeric and lemon grass form the basis of most rempah or spice paste.

Singapore Laksa

Serves 4–6

For the spice paste

8 shallots, chopped

4 garlic cloves, chopped

40g/1½oz fresh root ginger, peeled and chopped

2 lemon grass stalks, chopped

6 candlenuts or macadamia nuts

4 dried red chillies, soaked until soft and seeded

30ml/2 tbsp dried prawns (shrimp), soaked until soft

5–10ml/1–2 tsp belacan

5–10ml/1–2 tsp sugar

15ml/1 tbsp vegetable oil

For the laksa

vegetable oil, for deep-frying

6 shallots, finely sliced

600ml/1 pint/2½ cups coconut milk

400ml/14fl oz/1⅔ cups chicken stock

90g/3½oz prawns (shrimp), shelled

90g/3½oz squid, trimmed and sliced

6–8 scallops

75g/3oz cockles, shelled

225g/8oz fresh rice noodles or dried rice vermicelli, soaked in lukewarm water until pliable

90g/3½oz beansprouts

salt and ground black pepper

a small bunch of fresh mint, roughly chopped, and chilli oil, to garnish

1 Using a mortar and pestle or food processor, grind all the ingredients for the spice paste mixture, apart from the oil. Bind the paste with the oil and set aside.

2 Heat enough oil in a wok to deep-fry. Add the shallots to the oil and deep-fry until crispy and golden. Drain and set aside.

3 Heat 30ml/2 tbsp vegetable oil in a large wok or heavy pan. Stir in the spice paste and cook over a low heat for 3–4 minutes, until fragrant. Add the coconut milk and chicken stock and bring to the boil, stirring all the time. Add the prawns, squid and scallops and simmer gently, for about 5–10 minutes, until cooked. Add the cockles at the last minute and season the broth with salt and pepper.

4 Ladle the noodles into individual bowls. Add the beansprouts and ladle over the broth and seafood, making sure the noodles are submerged in the steaming liquid. Garnish with the crispy shallots, mint and a drizzle of chilli oil.

There are as many laksa dishes as there are regions in Malaysia and Singapore. The basic dish consists of noodles in a spicy coconut broth. In the home-cooked Singapore laksa, slices of deep-fried fish cakes are often added at the end, whereas the stall version is rich in a variety of seafood, topped with cockles.

Spicy Chicken Soup Soto ayam

Serves 6

1 small chicken, about 900g/2lb
2 lemon grass stalks, bruised
25g/1oz fresh root ginger, peeled
    and sliced
2 fresh kaffir lime leaves
1 dried red chilli
30ml/2 tbsp vegetable oil
50g/2oz mung bean thread noodles,
    soaked in lukewarm water until
    pliable, and drained
3 hard-boiled eggs, peeled and
    halved
115g/4oz beansprouts
a small bunch of fresh coriander
    (cilantro), roughly chopped, to
    garnish
2 limes, quartered, chilli oil and soy
    sauce, to serve

For the rempah

8 shallots, chopped
8 garlic cloves, chopped
6 candlenuts or macadamia nuts
50g/2oz galangal, chopped
2 lemon grass stalks, chopped
4 fresh kaffir lime leaves
15ml/1 tbsp ground coriander
10ml/2 tsp ground turmeric
15ml/1 tbsp vegetable oil

1 Using a mortar and pestle or a food processor, grind all the rempah ingredients to a paste. Set aside.

2 Put the chicken, lemon grass, ginger, lime leaves and chilli into a deep pan and pour in enough water to just cover. Bring to the boil, reduce the heat, cover and simmer for about 1 hour, until the chicken is tender. Remove the chicken from the stock, take off and discard the skin and tear the meat into shreds. Strain the stock.

3 In a wok or heavy pan, heat the oil. Stir in the rempah and cook for 1–2 minutes, until fragrant. Pour in the stock and stir well. Season to taste with salt and pepper.

4 Divide the noodles among six bowls. Add the hard-boiled eggs, beansprouts and shredded chicken. Ladle the steaming broth into each bowl and garnish with coriander. Serve immediately with the lime wedges, chilli oil and soy sauce to squeeze, drizzle and pour over it.

This fragrant soup is particularly popular in Singapore. Originally from Java, various versions are served at soup and noodle stalls specializing in Indonesian and Malay food. As many Malay Singaporeans came from Indonesia, it is always in demand. When served as a meal on its own, deep-fried potato fritters or chips (French fries), or the Malay compressed rice cakes, ketupat, accompany the soup.

Sweet and Sour Deep-fried Squid
Sotong goreng

Serves 4
900g/2lb fresh young, tender squid
vegetable oil, for deep-frying

For the marinade
60ml/4 tbsp light soy sauce
15ml/1 tbsp sugar

For the dipping sauce
30ml/2 tbsp tomato ketchup
15ml/1 tbsp Worcestershire sauce
15ml/1 tbsp light soy sauce
15ml/1 tbsp vegetable or sesame oil
sugar or honey, to sweeten
chilli oil, to taste

1 First prepare the squid. Hold the body in one hand and pull off the head with the other. Sever the tentacles and discard the rest. Remove the backbone and clean the body sack inside and out. Pat dry using kitchen paper and cut into rings.

2 In a bowl, mix the soy sauce with the sugar until it dissolves. Toss in the squid rings and tentacles and leave to marinate for 1 hour.

3 Meanwhile prepare the sauce. Mix together the tomato ketchup, Worcestershire sauce, soy sauce and oil. Sweeten with sugar or honey to taste and add as much chilli oil as you like. Set aside.

4 Heat enough oil for deep-frying in a wok or heavy pan. Thoroughly drain the squid of any marinade, pat with kitchen paper to avoid spitting, and fry until golden and crispy. Pat dry on kitchen paper and serve immediately with the dipping sauce.

COOK'S TIP
To avoid the spitting fat, lightly coat the squid in flour before deep-frying. Alternatively, fry in a deep-fat fryer with a lid or use a spatterproof cover on the wok or pan.

A favourite at the Singapore hawker stalls, deep-fried squid served with a sweet and sour sauce is popular with the Malays, Chinese, Peranakans and Eurasians. This is an example of a dish where the Western influence comes into play – with tomato ketchup and Worcestershire sauce.

Spicy Lentil and Meat Patties
Shami kebabs

1 Put the lentils in a pan and cover with plenty of water. Bring to a gentle boil and cook until they have softened but still have a bite to them – this can take 20–40 minutes depending on the type of lentil. Drain well.

2 Heat the oil in a heavy pan and stir in the onions, garlic, chilli and ginger. Fry until they begin to colour, then add the lentils and minced lamb. Cook for a few minutes, then add the curry powder and turmeric. Season with salt and pepper and cook the mixture over a high heat until the moisture has evaporated. The mixture needs to be dry for the patties.

3 Leave the meat mixture aside until it is cool enough to handle. Beat one of the eggs in a bowl and mix it into the meat. Using your fingers, take small portions of the mixture and roll them into balls about the size of a plum. Press each ball in the palm of your hand to form thick, flat patties – if the mixture is sticky, wet your palms with a little water.

4 Beat the remaining eggs in a bowl. Heat enough oil in a heavy pan for shallow frying. Dip each patty in the beaten egg and place them all into the oil. Fry for about 3–4 minutes each side until golden. Garnish with fresh coriander and serve with lemon wedges to squeeze over.

These lentil and lamb patties are popular on the Malay and Muslim stalls, which are often grouped together. Although of Indian origin, the shami kebabs of Malaysia and Singapore have been adapted to suit the local tastes, often served with rice and a sambal, or even between chunks of bread with tomato ketchup, like a burger.

Serves 4

150g/5oz/generous ½ cup red, brown, yellow or green lentils, rinsed
30ml/2 tbsp vegetable oil
2 onions, finely chopped
2 garlic cloves, finely chopped
1 green chilli, seeded and finely chopped
25g/1oz fresh root ginger, finely chopped
250g/9oz lean minced (ground) lamb
10ml/2 tsp Indian curry powder
5ml/1 tsp turmeric powder
4 eggs
vegetable oil, for shallow frying
salt and ground black pepper
fresh coriander (cilantro) leaves, roughly chopped, to garnish
1 lemon, quartered, to serve

Chargrilled Spicy Chicken Wings
Ayam panggang

1 First make the spice paste. Using a mortar and pestle or food processor, grind the shallots, garlic, ginger, chillies and lemon grass to a paste.

2 Bind with the oil and stir in the tomato purée, sugar and lime juice. Season with salt and pepper.

3 Rub the spice paste into the chicken wings, cover and leave to marinate for 2 hours.

4 Prepare the charcoal grill. Lift the wings out of the marinade and place them on the rack. Cook them for about 5 minutes each side until cooked through, brushing with marinade while they cook. Serve immediately, garnished with coriander and chillies.

Serves 4

12 chicken wings
fresh coriander (cilantro) leaves,
  roughly chopped, and 2–3 green
  chillies, seeded and quartered
  lengthways, to garnish

For the spice paste

4 shallots, chopped
4 garlic cloves, chopped
25g/1oz fresh root ginger, chopped
8 red chillies, seeded and chopped
1 lemon grass stalk, trimmed and
  chopped
30ml/2 tbsp sesame or groundnut
  (peanut) oil
15ml/1 tbsp tomato purée (paste)
10ml/2 tsp sugar
juice of 2 limes
salt and ground black pepper

Whole chickens or just the wings and drumsticks, marinated in spicy or tangy pastes and then grilled over charcoal or fried, are a common sight in the food stalls of Malaysia and Singapore. Spicy wings and drumsticks are very popular as a quick snack, which can even be enjoyed on the move.

They are often served on their own with a few sprigs of coriander and slices of chilli to munch on, or they form part of the wide selection of dishes on display at the tze char *stalls, where people fill their bowls with whatever they want.*

Malay Beehoon

Serves 4

30ml/2 tbsp vegetable oil

1 carrot, cut into matchsticks

225g/8oz fresh prawns (shrimp), peeled

120ml/4fl oz/½ cup chicken stock or water

30ml/2 tbsp light soy sauce

15ml/1 tbsp dark soy sauce

175g/6oz beansprouts

115g/4oz mustard greens or pak choi (bok choy), shredded

225g/8oz dried rice vermicelli, soaked in lukewarm water until pliable, and drained

1–2 fresh red chillies, seeded and finely sliced, and fresh coriander (cilantro) leaves, roughly chopped, to garnish

For the rempah

4 dried red chillies, soaked until soft and seeded

4 garlic cloves, chopped

4 shallots, chopped

25g/1oz fresh root ginger, peeled and chopped

5ml/1 tsp ground turmeric

1 Using a mortar and pestle or food processor, grind the ingredients for the rempah to a paste.

2 Heat the oil in a wok or heavy pan, and stir in the rempah until it begins to colour and become fragrant. Toss in the carrot for a minute, followed by the prawns. Pour in the stock or water and soy sauces and cook for 1 minute.

3 Add the beansprouts and mustard greens, followed by the noodles. Toss well to make sure the vegetables noodles are well coated and heated through. Transfer to a serving plate and garnish with the sliced chillies and coriander.

In Malaysia and Singapore, there are endless stir-fried noodle dishes. Some of these are classic Chinese recipes; others have been influenced by the Chinese but adapted to suit the tastes of the different communities. Beehoon is the Malay name for the rice vermicelli which, in this popular snack, are stir-fried with prawns and lots of chilli.

Singapore Egg Noodles Hokkein mee

Serves 4

30ml/2 tbsp vegetable oil

3 garlic cloves, finely chopped

115g/4oz pork fillet, cut into thin strips

115g/4oz fresh fish fillets (such as red snapper, grouper or trout), cut into bitesize pieces

115g/4oz fresh prawns (shrimp), shelled and deveined

2 small squid, with innards and backbone removed, cleaned and sliced (reserve tentacles)

300ml/½ pint/1¼ cups chicken stock

450g/1lb fresh egg noodles

1 carrot, shredded

6 long white Chinese cabbage leaves, shredded

30ml/2 tbsp dark soy sauce

30ml/2 tbsp light soy sauce

ground black pepper

a small bunch of fresh coriander (cilantro), roughly chopped

1 Heat the oil in a wok and stir in the garlic. When it becomes fragrant, stir in the pork, fish, prawns and squid, tossing them around the pan for 1 minute. Pour in the stock and bubble it up to reduce it.

2 Add the noodles and toss them around the wok for 1 minute. Stir in the shredded carrot and cabbage, add the soy sauces and cook until most of the liquid has evaporated. Season with pepper, sprinkle with the chopped, fresh coriander, divide the noodles among four bowls and eat steaming hot.

This is a very popular stir-fried dish in Singapore, where the majority of the Chinese population is Hokkein. The dish takes its name from the people, as well as from the thick egg noodles, called Hokkein noodles. Filled with squid, prawns, fish and pork, this is a satisfying meal in itself.

Chinese Clay Pot Rice with Chicken So po ayam

1 In a bowl, mix together the ingredients for the marinade. Toss in the chicken, making sure it is well coated. Set aside.

2 Make sure the shiitake mushrooms are soft (leave them to soak for longer, if necessary). Squeeze them to get rid of any excess water. Using a sharp knife, remove any hard stems and halve the caps. Add the mushroom caps and the Chinese sausage to the chicken.

3 Bring the stock to the boil in the clay pot. Stir in the rice and bring it back to the boil. Reduce the heat, cover the pot, and simmer on a low heat for 15–20 minutes, until almost all the liquid has been absorbed.

4 Spread the marinated mixture over the top of the rice and cover the pot. Leave to steam for about 10–15 minutes, until all the liquid is absorbed and the chicken is cooked. Garnish with coriander and serve.

COOK'S TIP
Remember, if you are using a newly bought clay pot, you need to treat it first. Fill it with water and slowly bring it to the boil. Simmer for 5–10 minutes, then leave it to cool. Pour out the water and wipe the pot dry. Now it is ready to use.

This Cantonese dish is a great family one-pot meal. It can also be found on Chinese stalls and in some coffee shops. The traditional clay pot ensures that the ingredients remain moist, while allowing the flavours to mingle, but any earthenware pot will do. This recipe also works well with prawns or strips of pork fillet.

Serves 4

500g/1¼lb chicken breast fillets, cut into thin strips

5 dried shiitake mushrooms, soaked in hot water for 30 minutes, until soft

1 Chinese sausage, sliced

750ml/1¼ pints/3 cups chicken stock

225g/8oz/generous 1 cup long grain rice, washed and drained

fresh coriander (cilantro) leaves, finely chopped, to garnish

For the marinade

30ml/2 tbsp sesame oil

45ml/3 tbsp oyster sauce

30ml/2 tbsp soy sauce

25g/1oz fresh root ginger, finely grated (shredded)

2 spring onions (scallions), trimmed and finely sliced

1 red chilli, seeded and finely sliced

5ml/1 tsp sugar

ground black pepper

Grilled Stingray Wings with Chilli Sambal
Ikan pari panggang

Serves 4

4 medium-sized stingray wings,
    about 200g/7oz, rinsed and dried
salt
4 banana leaves, about 30cm/12in
    square
2 fresh limes, quartered

For the chilli sambal

6–8 red chillies, seeded and chopped
4 garlic cloves, chopped
5ml/1 tsp shrimp paste
15ml/1 tbsp tomato purée (paste)
15ml/1 tbsp palm sugar
juice of 2 limes
30ml/2 tbsp vegetable or groundnut
    (peanut) oil

1 First make the chilli sambal. Using a mortar and pestle or food processor, grind the chillies with the garlic to form a paste. Beat in the shrimp paste, tomato purée and palm sugar. Add the lime juice and bind with the oil.

2 Prepare a charcoal grill. Rub each stingray wing with a little chilli sambal and place them on the rack.

3 Cook for 3–4 minutes on each side, until tender. Sprinkle with salt and serve on banana leaves with the remaining chilli sambal and the lime quarters.

Chargrilled stingray is a much-loved street snack in Singapore. The stalls selling chicken wings and satay often serve grilled stingray wings on a banana leaf with a generous dollop of chilli sambal. The cooked fish is eaten with fingers, or chopsticks, by tearing off pieces and dipping them in the sambal. If you can't find stingray wings, you could substitute a flat fish, such as plaice. Banana leaves are available in Chinese and Asian markets.

Indian Dry Prawn and Potato Curry
Gulai udang

Serves 4

30ml/2 tbsp ghee, or 15ml/1 tbsp
    vegetable oil and 15g/½oz/1 tbsp
    butter
1 onion, halved lengthways and
    sliced along the grain
a handful of fresh or dried curry
    leaves
1 cinnamon stick
2–3 medium-size waxy potatoes,
    lightly steamed, peeled and diced
500g/1¼lb fresh large prawns
    (shrimp), peeled and deveined
200ml/7fl oz/scant 1 cup coconut
    milk
10ml/2 tsp fennel seeds
10ml/2 tsp brown mustard seeds
salt and ground black pepper
fresh coriander (cilantro) leaves,
    roughly chopped, to garnish

For the spice paste

4 garlic cloves, chopped
25g/1oz fresh root ginger, peeled
    and chopped
2 red chillies, seeded and chopped
5ml/1 tsp ground turmeric
15ml/1 tbsp fish curry powder

1 First make the spice paste. Using a mortar and pestle or food processor, grind the garlic, ginger and chillies to a coarse paste. Stir in the turmeric and curry powder.

2 Heat the ghee in a heavy pan or earthenware pot. Stir in the onion and fry until golden. Stir in the curry leaves, followed by the cinnamon stick and the spice paste. Fry until fragrant, then add the potatoes, coating them in the spices. Toss in the prawns and cook for 12 minutes. Stir in the coconut milk and bubble it up to thicken and reduce it. Season with salt and pepper to taste.

3 Roast the fennel and mustard seeds in a small heavy pan until they begin to pop and give off a nutty aroma. Stir them into the curry and serve immediately, sprinkled with a little coriander.

This delicious dish is one of the most popular curries at the Indian stalls in Singapore. Generally, in an Indian home, this curry would be served with flatbread, a yogurt dish and chutney – dry curries are easy to scoop up with the bread – but, at the nasi kandar stalls, it is often one of several curried dishes served with rice. It's equally delicious made with pre-cooked sweet potatoes instead of ordinary ones.

Singapore Chilli Crab

1 Using a mortar and pestle or food processor, grind the ingredients for the spice paste and set aside.

2 Heat enough oil for deep-frying in a wok or heavy pan. Drop in the crabs and fry until the shells turn bright red. Remove the crabs from the oil and drain.

3 Heat the sesame oil in a wok and stir in the spice paste. Fry until fragrant and stir in the chilli sauce, ketchup, soy sauce and sugar. Toss in the fried crab and coat well in the sauce. Pour in the chicken stock or water and bring to the boil. Reduce the heat and simmer for 5 minutes. Season the sauce to taste.

4 Pour in the eggs, stirring gently, to let them set in the sauce. Serve immediately, garnished with spring onions and coriander.

Serves 4

vegetable oil, for deep-frying
4 fresh crabs, about 250g/9oz each,
    cleaned
30ml/2 tbsp sesame oil
30–45ml/2–3 tbsp chilli sauce
45ml/3 tbsp tomato ketchup
15ml/1 tbsp soy sauce
15ml/1 tbsp sugar
250ml/8fl oz/1 cup chicken stock
    or water
2 eggs, beaten
salt and ground black pepper
2 spring onions (scallions), finely
    sliced, and fresh coriander
    (cilantro) leaves, finely chopped, to
    garnish

For the spice paste

4 garlic cloves, chopped
25g/1oz fresh root ginger, chopped
4 red chillies, seeded and chopped

Perhaps Singapore's signature dish could be chilli crab. An all-time favourite at hawker stalls and coffee shops, steaming woks of crab deep-frying are a common sight. Spicy and delicious, this is a dish where your fingers will get messy. The crabs are placed in the middle of the table with a bowl for the discarded pieces of shell, and small bowls of water for cleaning your fingers. Crack the shells, then dip the meat into the cooking sauce. Mop up the sauce with lots of crusty bread.

Pork Ribs in Pandanus Leaves Pandan babi

Serves 4–5
675g/1½lb meaty pork ribs, cut into
    bitesize pieces
25 pandanus (screwpine) leaves
vegetable oil, for deep-frying
2 limes, cut into wedges, to serve

For the marinade
6 shallots, chopped
4 garlic cloves, chopped
25g/1oz fresh root ginger, peeled
    and chopped
30ml/2 tbsp clear honey
45ml/3 tbsp Worcestershire sauce
30ml/2 tbsp tomato ketchup
30ml/2 tbsp sour plum sauce
15ml/1 tbsp sesame oil

1 First make the marinade. Using a mortar and pestle or food processor, grind the shallots, garlic and ginger to a smooth paste. Beat in the honey, Worcestershire sauce, tomato ketchup, sour plum sauce and sesame oil. Put the pork ribs in a shallow dish and smear the marinade all over them. Set aside for 2–3 hours.

2 Lay the pandanus leaves on a flat surface and place a marinated pork rib in the centre of each one. Tie a tight knot over each rib so that the ends poke out.

3 Heat enough oil in a wok or heavy pan for deep-frying and fry the wrapped ribs in batches for 4–5 minutes until cooked. Serve immediately with lime wedges, allowing each diner to untie the leaves and squeeze a splash of lime over the ribs.

USING OTHER LEAVES
Pandanus leaves emit a unique fragrance but you can instead use banana or bamboo leaves cut into strips.

The Malays have a penchant for sweet tastes and pork is often married with sweet flavourings. The Dyaks love their pork coated in honey and grilled, stir-fried or roasted. In this Chinese-style Singapore dish, the pork is marinated in honey and Western flavourings, before being wrapped in the long, thin pandanus leaves and deep-fried. Serve the pork ribs as an appetizer or as a main course with stir-fried rice or noodles.

Singapore Five-spice Meat Rolls

1 Put the minced pork, chopped prawns and water chestnuts in a bowl. Add the soy sauces, sour plum sauce and sesame oil and mix well. Stir in the five-spice powder, glutinous rice flour or cornflour, and egg. Mix together well.

2 Lay the tofu sheets on a flat surface and divide the minced pork mixture between them, placing spoonfuls towards the edge nearest you. Pull the nearest edge up over the filling, tuck in the sides and carefully roll into a log, just like a spring roll. Moisten the last edge with a little water to seal the roll.

3 Fill a wok one-third of the way up with water and place a bamboo steamer into it. Heat the water and place the tofu rolls in the steamer. Cover and steam for 15 minutes. Remove the steamed rolls with tongs and place them on a clean dishtowel.

4 Heat enough oil for deep-frying in a wok. Fry the steamed rolls in batches until crisp and golden. Drain them on kitchen paper and serve whole or sliced into portions. Drizzle with chilli oil and serve with a bowl of soy sauce mixed with chopped chillies for dipping.

COOK'S TIP
If you cannot find tofu sheets, try the recipe with Asian rice sheets or Middle Eastern filo pastry.

Serves 4

225g/8oz minced (ground) pork
150g/5oz fresh prawns (shrimp), peeled and finely chopped
115g/4oz water chestnuts, finely chopped
15ml/1 tbsp light soy sauce
15ml/1 tbsp dark soy sauce
15ml/1 tbsp sour plum sauce
7.5ml/1½ tsp sesame oil
10ml/2 tsp Chinese five-spice powder
5ml/1 tsp glutinous rice flour or cornflour (cornstarch)
1 egg, lightly beaten
4 fresh tofu sheets, 18–20cm/7–8in square, soaked in warm water
vegetable oil, for deep-frying
chilli oil, for drizzling
soy sauce mixed with chopped chillies, to serve

A great favourite at the cze cha hawker stalls in Singapore, these deep-fried steamed rolls are delicious with a dipping sauce. Wrapped in the traditional tofu sheets, the light, tasty rolls can be served as a snack, an appetizer or as a light meal with rice and a vegetable dish or salad. Fresh tofu sheets are available in Chinese and Asian markets.

Serves 4

2 shallots, chopped
4 garlic cloves, chopped
50g/2oz fresh root ginger or
    galangal, peeled and chopped
25g/1oz fresh turmeric, chopped
2 lemon grass stalks, chopped
12 chicken thighs or drumsticks or
    6 whole chicken legs, separated
    into drumsticks and thighs
30ml/2 tbsp kecap manis
salt and ground black pepper
vegetable oil, for deep-frying

Malaysian Fried Chicken
Ayam goreng

1 Using a mortar and pestle or food processor, grind the shallots, garlic, ginger or galangal, turmeric and lemon grass to a paste.

2 Place the chicken pieces in a heavy pan or earthenware pot and smear with the spice paste. Add the kecap manis and 150ml/¼ pint/⅔ cup water. Bring to the boil, reduce the heat and cook the chicken for about 25 minutes, turning it from time to time, until the liquid has evaporated. The chicken should be dry before deep-frying, but the spices should be sticking to it. Season with salt and pepper.

3 Heat enough oil for deep-frying in a wok. Fry the chicken pieces in batches until golden brown and crisp. Drain them on kitchen paper and serve hot.

TO SERVE

Served with a sambal, or pickle, ayam goreng makes a delicious snack, but for a main course, serve with yellow or fragrant coconut rice and a salad. If you cannot find kecap manis, use soy sauce sweetened with palm sugar, available in Chinese and Asian markets, or substitute the same quantity of dark soy sauce and 15ml/1 tbsp sugar.

You cannot visit Malaysia or Singapore without trying the famous fried chicken. Indonesian in origin, ayam goreng puts Western fried chicken to shame. First the chicken is cooked in spices and flavourings to ensure a depth of taste, then it is simply deep-fried to form a crisp, golden skin.

Malay Braised Duck in Aromatic Soy Sauce
Teochew duck

Serves 4–6

1 duck (about 2kg/4½lb), washed
  and trimmed
15–30ml/1–2 tbsp Chinese five-
  spice powder
25g/1oz fresh turmeric, chopped
25g/1oz galangal, chopped
4 garlic cloves, chopped
30ml/2 tbsp sesame oil
12 shallots, peeled and left whole
2–3 lemon grass stalks, halved and
  lightly crushed
4 cinnamon sticks
8 star anise
12 cloves
600ml/1 pint/2½ cups light soy
  sauce
120ml/4fl oz/½ cup dark soy sauce
30–45ml/2–3 tbsp palm sugar
fresh coriander (cilantro) leaves, 2
  green and 2 red chillies, seeded
  and quartered lengthways, to
  garnish
steamed jasmine rice and salad, to
  serve

1 Rub the duck, inside and out, with the five-spice powder and place in the refrigerator, uncovered, for 6–8 hours.

2 Using a mortar and pestle or food processor, grind the turmeric, galangal and garlic to a smooth paste. Heat the oil in a heavy pan and stir in the spice paste until it becomes fragrant. Stir in the shallots, lemon grass, cinnamon sticks, star anise and cloves. Pour in the soy sauces and stir in the palm sugar until dissolved.

3 Place the duck in the pan, baste with the sauce, and add 550ml/18fl oz/2½ cups water. Bring to the boil, reduce the heat and cover the pan. Simmer gently for 4–6 hours, basting from time to time, until the duck is very tender. Garnish with coriander and chillies, and serve with rice and salad.

The Chinese communities in Malaysia and Singapore often braise duck, goose, chicken or pork in soy sauce and warm flavourings, such as star anise and cinnamon. Such dishes are found at Chinese hawker stalls and coffee shops, and there are many variations on the theme. The Malays like to add turmeric and lemon grass to the flavourings and, to achieve their desired fiery kick, chillies are always tucked into the recipe somewhere.

Deep-fried Aubergine with Garlic Sauce Terung sambal

Serves 2–4

6 shallots, chopped
4 garlic cloves, chopped
2 red chillies, seeded and chopped
1 lemon grass stalk, trimmed and
   chopped
5ml/1 tsp shrimp paste
15ml/1 tbsp sesame oil
15–30ml/1–2 tbsp soy sauce
7.5ml/1½ tsp sugar
2 slender, purple aubergines
   (eggplants), partially peeled in
   strips and halved lengthways
vegetable oil, for deep-frying

To garnish

1 green chilli, seeded and finely
   chopped
a small bunch each of fresh mint and
   coriander (cilantro), stalks
   removed, finely chopped

1 Using a mortar and pestle or food processor, grind the shallots, garlic, chillies and lemon grass to a paste. Beat in the shrimp paste and mix well.

2 Heat the sesame oil in a small wok or heavy pan. Stir in the spice paste and cook until fragrant and brown. Stir in the soy sauce and sugar and cook until smooth. Remove from the heat.

3 Heat enough oil for deep-frying in a wok or heavy pan. Drop in the aubergine halves and fry until tender. Drain on kitchen paper, then press down the centre of each half to make a dip or shallow pouch.

4 Arrange the aubergine halves on a plate and smear with the spicy sauce. Garnish with the chopped green chilli, mint and coriander and serve at room temperature.

This dish is often served at the rice stalls in Singapore as an accompaniment to a main rice dish such as nasi lemak, Malay coconut rice. Many cooks at the stalls, and in the home, make up batches of different sambals to be stored and used for quick dishes like this one. Generally, the aubergines are deep-fried at the hawker stalls, but you could bake them in the oven at home. Serve as a snack with bread or as a side dish to rice or grilled meats.

Nonya Cabbage in Coconut Milk
Kubis masak lemak

1 Using a mortar and pestle or food processor, grind the shallots, garlic, lemon grass, ginger and chillies to a paste. Beat in the shrimp paste, turmeric and sugar.

2 Heat the oil in a wok or heavy pan, and stir in the spice paste. Cook until fragrant and beginning to colour.

3 Pour in the coconut milk, mix well, and bubble it up to thicken. Drop in the cabbage leaves, coating them in the coconut milk, and cook for a minute or two until wilted. Season to taste and serve immediately.

Serves 4

4 shallots, chopped
2 garlic cloves, chopped
1 lemon grass stalk, trimmed and
   chopped
25g/1oz fresh root ginger, peeled
   and chopped
2 red chillies, seeded and chopped
5ml/1 tsp shrimp paste
5ml/1 tsp turmeric powder
5ml/1 tsp palm sugar
15ml/1 tbsp sesame or groundnut
   (peanut) oil
400ml/14fl oz/1⅔ cups coconut milk
450g/1lb Chinese leaves (Chinese
   cabbage) or kale, cut into thick
   ribbons, or pak choi (bok choy),
   separated into leaves, or a mixture
   of the two
salt and ground black pepper

In Melaka and Johor, where the culinary culture is influenced by the Chinese, Malay, and Peranakans, it is no wonder that Nonya cuisine blooms. With good agricultural ground, there is an abundance of vegetables that, in this part of Malaysia, are often cooked in coconut milk. For this dish, you could use green beans, curly kale, or any type of cabbage, all of which are delicious served with steamed, braised or grilled fish dishes.

Potato Curry with Yogurt Potato korma

Serves 4

6 garlic cloves, chopped

25g/1oz fresh root ginger, peeled and chopped

30ml/2 tbsp ghee, or 15ml/1 tbsp oil and 15g/½oz/1 tbsp butter

6 shallots, halved lengthways and sliced along the grain

2 green chillies, seeded and finely sliced

10ml/2 tsp sugar

a handful of fresh or dried curry leaves

2 cinnamon sticks

5–10ml/1–2 tsp ground turmeric

15ml/1 tbsp garam masala

500g/1¼lb waxy potatoes, cut into bitesize pieces

2 tomatoes, peeled, seeded and quartered

250ml/8fl oz/1 cup Greek (US strained plain) yogurt

salt and ground black pepper

5ml/1 tsp red chilli powder, and fresh coriander (cilantro) and mint leaves, finely chopped, to garnish

1 lemon, quartered, to serve

1 Using a mortar and pestle or a food processor, grind the garlic and ginger to a coarse paste. Heat the ghee in a heavy pan and stir in the shallots and chillies, until fragrant. Add the garlic and ginger paste with the sugar, and stir until the mixture begins to colour. Stir in the curry leaves, cinnamon sticks, turmeric and garam masala, and toss in the potatoes, making sure they are coated in the spice mixture.

2 Pour in just enough cold water to cover the potatoes. Bring to the boil, then reduce the heat and simmer until the potatoes are just cooked – they should still have a bite to them.

3 Season with salt and pepper to taste. Gently toss in the tomatoes to heat them through. Fold in the yogurt so that it is streaky rather than completely mixed in. Sprinkle with the chilli powder, coriander and mint. Serve immediately from the pan, with lemon to squeeze over it and flatbread for scooping it up.

VARIATION

This recipe also works well with sweet potatoes, butternut squash or pumpkin, all of which absorb the flavours.

Variations of this simple Indian curry are to be found at Malay and Muslim stalls, and at roti stalls, where it is served with flatbread. Some of the Singapore coffee shops even serve it for breakfast. Generally, the Malays and Indians serve this dish with a meat curry and rice, but it is also delicious on its own, served with yogurt and a spicy pickle or chutney. A dry version, without yogurt, is used as a filling for some of the tasty flatbreads and savoury pastries sold at the hawker stalls in Singapore.

Winter Melon Pachadi

Serves 4

225g/8oz winter melon, peeled,
seeded and diced
5ml/1 tsp ground turmeric
5ml/1 tsp red chilli powder
300ml/½ pint/1¼ cups Greek
(US strained plain) yogurt
2.5ml/½ tsp salt
2.5ml/½ tsp sugar
15g/½ oz fresh root ginger, peeled
and grated
1 green chilli, seeded and finely
chopped
15ml/1 tbsp vegetable oil
1.5ml/¼ tsp ground asafoetida
5ml/1 tsp brown mustard seeds
8–10 dried curry leaves
1 dried red chilli, seeded and
roughly chopped

1 Put the winter melon in a heavy pan with the turmeric and chilli powder and pour in enough water to just cover. Bring to the boil and cook gently, uncovered, until the winter melon is tender and all the water has evaporated.

2 In a bowl, beat the yogurt with the salt and sugar until smooth and creamy. Add the ginger and green chilli, and fold in the warm winter melon.

3 Heat the oil in small heavy pan. Stir in the asafoetida and the mustard seeds. As soon as the mustard seeds begin to pop, stir in the curry leaves and dried chilli. When the chilli darkens, add the spices to the melon and mix thoroughly. Serve at room temperature.

This pachadi dish, originally from southern India, is designed to cool the palate and aid digestion when eating hot, spicy food.

Rojak

Serves 4–6

1 jicama (sweet turnip), peeled and
finely sliced
1 small cucumber, partially peeled
and finely sliced
1 green mango, peeled and finely
sliced
1 star fruit (carambola), finely sliced
4 slices fresh pineapple, cored
half a pomelo, separated into
segments, membrane removed
a handful of beansprouts, rinsed
and drained
fresh mint leaves, to garnish

For the sauce

225g/8oz/2 cups roasted peanuts
4 garlic cloves, chopped
2–4 red chillies, seeded and chopped
10ml/2 tsp shrimp paste, dry-roasted
in a pan over a high heat
15ml/1 tbsp tamarind paste
30ml/2 tbsp palm sugar
salt

*This recipe is so flexible, you
can use any combination of
fruit and vegetables and
make the sauce as pungent
and fiery as you like.*

1 First make the sauce. Using a mortar and pestle or food processor, grind the peanuts with the garlic and chillies to a coarse paste. Beat in the roasted shrimp paste, tamarind paste and sugar. Add enough water to make a thick, pouring sauce, and stir until the sugar has dissolved. Add salt to taste.

2 Arrange the sliced fruit and vegetables on a plate, with the beansprouts scattered over the top. Drizzle the sauce over the salad and garnish with mint leaves. Serve with grilled meats and spicy dishes, or on its own as a healthy snack.

Jellied Mango Puddings with Tropical Fruits

Serves 4

750ml/1¼ pints/3 cups coconut milk
150g/5oz/¾ cup sugar
15ml/1 tbsp powdered gelatine
 (gelatin)
1 egg yolk
1 large, ripe mango, stoned (pitted)
 and puréed
4 slices ripe jackfruit or pineapple,
 quartered
1 banana, cut into diagonal slices
1 kiwi fruit, sliced
4 lychees, peeled
2 passion fruit, split open, to decorate

1 In a heavy pan, heat the coconut milk with the sugar, stirring all the time, until it has dissolved. Add the gelatine and keep stirring until it has dissolved. Remove from the heat. Beat the egg yolk with the mango purée. Add the purée to the coconut milk and stir until smooth. Spoon the mixture into individual, lightly oiled moulds and leave to cool. Place them in the refrigerator for 2–3 hours, until set.

2 To serve, arrange the fruit on individual plates, leaving enough room for the jellies. Dip the base of each mould briefly into hot water, and then invert the puddings on to the plates. Lift off the moulds and decorate with passion fruit seeds.

VARIATION
The tangy fruitiness of mango is particularly delicious in these jellied puddings, but you could substitute papaya, banana, durian or avocado.

Light and sophisticated, these jellied mango puddings make delightful desserts. Served with a selection of tropical fruits, they add a refreshing touch to the end of a spicy meal. You are more likely to find these elegant little puddings in the dim sum restaurants in Singapore and Kuala Lumpur than as a sweet snack at a hawker stall.

Deep-fried Bananas with Coconut

1 Sift the flour with the baking powder and a pinch of salt into a bowl. Make a well in the centre and drop in the eggs. Gradually pour in the coconut milk, beating all the time, until the batter is thick and smooth.

2 Beat in the sugar and fresh desiccated coconut and add the banana pieces, coating them gently with the batter.

3 Heat enough oil for deep-frying in a wok or large heavy pan. Check the oil is the right temperature by dropping in a cube of bread – if it sizzles and turns golden brown, the oil is ready. Lift the pieces of banana out of the batter with tongs or chopsticks and lower them into the oil. Fry two or three pieces at a time, until crisp and golden, and drain on kitchen paper. Repeat with the remaining banana pieces. Sprinkle sugar over the bananas and serve while still warm.

Serves 4–6

115g/4oz/1 cup plain (all-purpose) or rice flour
5ml/1 tsp baking powder
2 eggs
750ml/1¼ pints/3 cups coconut milk
30ml/2 tbsp palm or granulated sugar
90g/3½oz fresh coconut, grated or desiccated (dry unsweetened shredded) coconut
3 large bananas, halved widthways and lengthways
vegetable oil, for deep-frying
salt
caster (superfine) or icing (confectioners') sugar, for sprinkling

Perhaps the most common of all the sweet snacks, deep-fried bananas are eaten throughout South-east Asia, and are a hawker-stall favourite. Versatile and tasty, they are often munched on their own, sprinkled with sugar, or they can be served with sweet sticky rice, ice creams or steamed cakes and buns.

Roasted Coconut Ice Cream

Serves 4–6

115g/4oz fresh coconut, finely
   chopped in a food processor
4 large (US extra large) egg yolks
115g/4oz/generous ½ cup caster
   (superfine) sugar
900ml/1½ pints/3¾ cups coconut
   milk
250ml/8fl oz/1 cup double (heavy)
   cream
25ml/1½ tbsp rice flour, blended
   with 30ml/2 tbsp coconut milk or
   cream
salt

The popularity of ice cream in Malaysia and Singapore ensures that, in the cities at least, you will not have to search for it. Ice cream trucks set themselves up at busy street corners selling an exotic selection, with flavours ranging from passion fruit, mango, sour plum and durian to coconut, avocado and corn.

1 Gently roast the coconut in a heavy frying pan until nicely browned and emitting a nutty aroma. Transfer to a plate and leave to cool.

2 In a bowl, whisk the egg yolks with the sugar until pale and creamy. In a heavy pan, heat the coconut milk with the cream and a pinch of salt to scalding point. Gradually pour the hot coconut milk into the egg yolk mixture, whisking at the same time to form a smooth custard. Strain the custard into a clean heavy pan and stir it gently until slightly thickened.

3 Beat the rice flour mixture into the custard until it coats the back of a spoon. Pour the custard into a freezer-proof container and leave to cool.

4 Stir most of the roasted coconut (reserve a little for decorating) into the cooled custard and put it in the freezer until frozen, taking it out and stirring after about half an hour. Alternatively, churn in an ice cream maker according to the manufacturer's instructions.

5 To serve, sprinkle the ice cream with the reserved roasted coconut.

Sweet Puréed Avocado

Serves 2

1 avocado, stoned (pitted)
juice of ½ lime
30ml/2 tbsp sweetened condensed
    milk
30ml/2 tbsp coconut cream
a pinch of salt
fresh mint leaves, to decorate
½ lime, halved, to serve

1 Put the avocado flesh into a food processor and purée it with the lime juice. Add the condensed milk, coconut cream and salt and process until the mixture is smooth and creamy.

2 Spoon the mixture into individual bowls or glasses and chill over ice. Decorate with a few mint leaves and serve with lime wedges to squeeze over it.

VARIATION

This recipe works equally well with other soft-fleshed fruit, such as bananas, mango and papaya.

This sweet avocado snack is thought to have originated with the Dutch in Melaka, but now it is also served in Penang and Singapore, where it is eaten by sweet-toothed Malays, Indians, and Eurasians. It can be served as a thick purée or blended with coconut milk until it is the consistency of thick pouring cream. It can also be enjoyed as a drink with a couple of ice cubes stirred in.

Singapore Sling

Serves 1

ice cubes
30ml/2 tbsp gin
15ml/1 tbsp grenadine
50ml/2fl oz/¼ cup sweet and sour
soda water
30ml/2 tbsp cherry brandy
1 maraschino cherry, to decorate

1 Place the ice cubes in a tall cocktail glass. Pour in the gin, grenadine and sweet and sour. Fill the glass up with soda water. Splash in the cherry brandy and top with the cherry. Serve immediately with a straw.

SWEET AND SOUR

This is also known as sour mix, sweet and sour mix, or bar mix. It is a mixer made of lemon or lime juice and sugar syrup and is an important part of many cocktails. To make your own, mix one part heavy sugar syrup (3 parts sugar, 2 parts water) with one part lemon juice, and add 2 egg whites per 1 litre/1¾ pints/4 cups of mix. The egg whites are optional; they will make the drinks slightly foamy. You may want to adjust the sugar/juice ratio for the right balance of sweetness and tartness.

Needless to say, this drink is from Singapore. However, it is not really drunk by the locals, who are largely Chinese, Peranakans, Muslim Malays and Hindu Indians. Some businessmen may partake in a beer or a glass of wine now and then, but cocktails like this are really for the tourists. It is on offer in every high-class hotel and restaurant; some even specialize in it.

Nutritional notes

Pineapple Pickle: Energy 56Kcal/238kJ; Protein 0.7g; Carbohydrate 12.5g, of which sugars 12.2g; Fat 0.2g, of which saturates 0g; Cholesterol 0mg; Calcium 20mg; Fibre 1.3g; Sodium 4mg.

Sambal Belacan: Energy 17Kcal/69kJ; Protein 2.8g; Carbohydrate 0.8g, of which sugars 0.8g; Fat 0.3g, of which saturates 0g; Cholesterol 19mg; Calcium 53mg; Fibre 0g; Sodium 312mg.

Singapore Laksa: Energy 300Kcal/1254kJ; Protein 14.2g; Carbohydrate 38g, of which sugars 6.9g; Fat 10.3g, of which saturates 1.4g; Cholesterol 77mg; Calcium 69mg; Fibre 0.7g; Sodium 211mg.

Spicy Chicken Soup: Energy 493Kcal/2050kJ; Protein 36g; Carbohydrate 8.5g, of which sugars 1g; Fat 35.1g, of which saturates 9.1g; Cholesterol 258mg; Calcium 47mg; Fibre 0.8g; Sodium 178mg.

Sweet and Sour Deep-fried Squid: Energy 315Kcal/1320kJ; Protein 35.2g; Carbohydrate 4.5g, of which sugars 1.7g; Fat 17.6g, of which saturates 2.5g; Cholesterol 506mg; Calcium 39mg; Fibre 0g; Sodium 1361mg.

Spicy Lentil and Meat Patties: Energy 488Kcal/2033kJ; Protein 28g; Carbohydrate 25.7g, of which sugars 3.7g; Fat 31.2g, of which saturates 7.4g; Cholesterol 238mg; Calcium 87mg; Fibre 3.1g; Sodium 140mg.

Chargrilled Spicy Chicken Wings: Energy 350Kcal/1455kJ; Protein 30.7g; Carbohydrate 2.6g, of which sugars 2.6g; Fat 24.1g, of which saturates 5.9g; Cholesterol 134mg; Calcium 11mg; Fibre 0.1g; Sodium 99mg.

Malay Beehoon: Energy 330Kcal/1377kJ; Protein 17.5g; Carbohydrate 49.9g, of which sugars 4.5g; Fat 6.6g, of which saturates 0.8g; Cholesterol 110mg; Calcium 125mg; Fibre 1.9g; Sodium 960mg.

Singapore Egg Noodles: Energy 609Kcal/2571kJ; Protein 35.2g; Carbohydrate 84.4g, of which sugars 5.3g; Fat 16.9g, of which saturates 3.8g; Cholesterol 186mg; Calcium 81mg; Fibre 4.2g; Sodium 867mg.

Chinese Clay Pot Rice with Chicken: Energy 371Kcal/1560kJ; Protein 36.2g; Carbohydrate 46.8g,

of which sugars 1g; Fat 4g, of which saturates 1.2g; Cholesterol 93mg; Calcium 54mg; Fibre 0.7g; Sodium 721mg.

Grilled Stingray Wings with Chilli Sambal. Energy 195Kcal/823kJ; Protein 30.4g; Carbohydrate 4.5g, of which sugars 4.5g; Fat 6.3g, of which saturates 0.7g; Cholesterol 0mg; Calcium 83mg; Fibre 0.1g; Sodium 249mg.

Indian Dry Prawn and Potato Curry: Energy 204Kcal/857kJ; Protein 23.5g; Carbohydrate 13.5g, of which sugars 5.2g; Fat 6.6g, of which saturates 0.9g; Cholesterol 244mg; Calcium 126mg; Fibre 1g; Sodium 299mg.

Singapore Chilli Crab: Energy 276Kcal/1144kJ; Protein 12.1g; Carbohydrate 8.6g, of which sugars 8.1g; Fat 21.7g, of which saturates 3.1g; Cholesterol 126mg; Calcium 23mg; Fibre 0.3g; Sodium 674mg.

Pork Ribs in Pandanus Leaves: Energy 299Kcal/1250kJ; Protein 25.5g; Carbohydrate 4.1g, of which sugars 3.8g; Fat 20.3g, of which saturates 7.3g; Cholesterol 89mg; Calcium 24mg; Fibre 0.2g; Sodium 182mg.

Singapore Five-spice Meat Rolls: Energy 339Kcal/1413kJ; Protein 24.4g; Carbohydrate 12.5g, of which sugars 2.7g; Fat 21.6g, of which saturates 4.2g; Cholesterol 158mg; Calcium 343mg; Fibre 1.2g; Sodium 665mg.

Malaysian Fried Chicken: Energy 396Kcal/1639kJ; Protein 27g; Carbohydrate 1.5g, of which sugars 1.1g; Fat 31.3g, of which saturates 6.8g; Cholesterol 150mg; Calcium 38mg; Fibre 0.2g; Sodium 358mg.

Malay Braised Duck in Aromatic Soy Sauce: Energy 119Kcal/498kJ; Protein 10.2g; Carbohydrate 4.6g, of which sugars 3.4g; Fat 6.9g, of which saturates 1.5g; Cholesterol 50mg; Calcium 35mg; Fibre 1.1g; Sodium 412mg.

Deep-fried Aubergine with Spicy Garlic Sauce: Energy 158Kcal/654kJ; Protein 1.6g; Carbohydrate 6.5g, of which sugars 5.1g; Fat 14.2g, of which saturates 1.8g; Cholesterol 0mg; Calcium 24mg; Fibre 2.7g; Sodium 271mg.

Nonya Cabbage in Coconut Milk: Energy 112Kcal/469kJ; Protein 2.1g; Carbohydrate 13g, of which sugars 12.6g; Fat 6.1g, of which saturates 1g; Cholesterol 0mg; Calcium 89mg; Fibre 2.6g; Sodium 119mg.

Potato Curry with Yogurt: Energy 231Kcal/967kJ; Protein 6.7g; Carbohydrate 26.2g, of which sugars 7.4g; Fat 12.4g, of which saturates 4.1g; Cholesterol 0mg; Calcium 110mg; Fibre 2g; Sodium 63mg.

Winter Melon Pachadi: Energy 127Kcal/527kJ; Protein 5.1g; Carbohydrate 5.3g, of which sugars 5.3g; Fat 10.5g, of which saturates 4.2g; Cholesterol 0mg; Calcium 120mg; Fibre 0.2g; Sodium 316mg.

Rojak: Energy 330Kcal/1381kJ; Protein 12.9g; Carbohydrate 28g, of which sugars 25.1g; Fat 19.3g, of which saturates 3.4g; Cholesterol 13mg; Calcium 114mg; Fibre 6.3g; Sodium 416mg.

Jellied Mango Puddings with Tropical Fruits: Energy 305Kcal/1300kJ; Protein 2.9g; Carbohydrate 72.6g, of which sugars 72g; Fat 2.4g, of which saturates 0.8g; Cholesterol 50mg; Calcium 109mg; Fibre 3g; Sodium 216mg.

Deep-fried Bananas with Coconut: Energy 377Kcal/1571kJ; Protein 5g; Carbohydrate 39.6g, of which sugars 22.7g; Fat 22.5g, of which saturates 9.9g; Cholesterol 63mg; Calcium 26mg; Fibre 3.2g; Sodium 30mg.

Roasted Coconut Ice Cream: Energy 448Kcal/1863kJ; Protein 4.1g; Carbohydrate 32.5g, of which sugars 29.1g; Fat 34.3g, of which saturates 21.9g; Cholesterol 192mg; Calcium 95mg; Fibre 1.8g; Sodium 191mg.

Sweet Puréed Avocado: Energy 243Kcal/1006kJ; Protein 3.2g; Carbohydrate 10.3g, of which sugars 9.2g; Fat 21.2g, of which saturates 8.5g; Cholesterol 5mg; Calcium 54mg; Fibre 2.6g; Sodium 421mg.

Singapore Sling: Energy 309Kcal/1296kJ; Protein 0g; Carbohydrate 35.5g, of which sugars 35.4g; Fat 0g, of which saturates 0g; Cholesterol 0mg; Calcium 3mg; Fibre 0g; Sodium 48mg.